THE TWO GENTLEMEN OF VERONA

LOVE LETTERS

"Sweet love, sweet lines, sweet life!"
PROTEUS 1,1

WHO'S THERE?

"Love is blind"
SPEED 2,1

FAIR PLAY

"One feast, one house, one mutual happiness"
VALENTINE 5,4

FRIENDS Valentine and Proteus both love Silvia, but Proteus already has a girlfriend called Julia. Eventually, all ends happily. Proteus marries Julia and Valentine marries Silvia. The two couples share the same wedding day.

THE TAMING OF THE SHREW

EARLY DAYS

"If I be waspish, best beware my sting"
KATE 2,1

BUDGE AN INCH

"He that knows better how to tame a shrew, / Now let him speak"
PETRUCHIO 4,1

TRUE LOVE

"Why, there's a wench! Come on, and kiss me, Kate"
PETRUCHIO 5,1

KATE has a reputation for upsetting people and her father won't let her sister, Bianca, marry until Kate is married herself. Petruchio manages to woo Kate. In the end, both sisters are married and Kate becomes a loyal wife to Petruchio.

TITUS ANDRONICUS

HARD-HEARTED

"I'll find a day to massacre them all"
TAMORA 1,1

FLESH AND BLOOD

"She hath no tongue to call, nor hands to wash"
DEMETRIUS 2,4

SHIVERING SHOCKS

"Why, there they are, both baked in this pie"
TITUS 5,3

TITUS wins a war against the Goths. The sons of Tamora, Queen of the Goths, attack Titus's daughter, Lavinia. He gets his revenge by baking her sons in a pie and feeding it to Tamora!

"...send... the...to...
...his last gasp"
JOAN OF ARC 1,2

AFTER Henry V dies, his young son becomes king. Some believe Henry is not the rightful king and Joan of Arc raises an army in France to free areas under English rule. Joan is captured and burned at the stake. Meanwhile, Henry marries a French lady in an attempt to secure his throne.

HENRY VI (Part 2)

YIELD THE CROWN

"I'll make him yield the crown, / Whose bookish rule hath pulled fair England down"
YORK 1,1

DANGEROUS DAYS

"The first thing we do, let's kill all the lawyers"
RIOTING BUTCHER 4,2

HAVING handed over land in France in order to marry Margaret of Anjou, Henry's power grows weaker. The Duke of York raises a rebel army to seize the crown for himself. The King and Queen flee the battlefield but York's soldiers chase them back to London.

HENRY VI (Part 3)

OFF WITH HIS HEAD!

"Off with the crown, and with the crown his head" MARGARET 1,4

IN A PICKLE

"O God! Methinks it were a happy life, / ...be no better than a homely swain, / To... upon a hill, as I do now"
HENRY VI 2,5

William Shakespeare, aged 26, is husband to Anne Hathaway and father to three children, Susanna and twins Hamnet and Judith.

1590

Philip Sidney's epic poem *Arcadia*, set in ancient Greece, is published. Shakespeare borrows from it for the Gloucester subplot in *King Lear*.

1591

Construction of the Rialto Bridge across the Grand Canal in Venice is completed.

1592

RICHARD III

STONY-HEARTED VILLAIN
"Plots have I laid, inductions dangerous"
RICHARD III 1.1

...ERIES TERRIBLE
"Break thou in pieces, and consume to ashes, / Thou foul accursed minister of hell!"
YORK 5.6

EDWARD IV is king, and his brother Richard plots against him to seize the crown. In the end, Richard's reign of terror is too much and his people turn against him. Richard is killed at Bosworth by Henry, Earl of Richmond, who then becomes king.

STRANGELY VISITED
"Bloody thou art, bloody will be thy end"
DUCHESS OF YORK 4.4

CREAM-FACED
"A horse! A horse! My kingdom for a horse!"
RICHARD III 5.4

RICHARD is an unpopular king and people want his cousin Bolingbroke to take his place. Richard gives up the crown rather than fight. Bolingbroke imprisons Richard and is crowned Henry IV. Richard is murdered.

DOUBLE-DEALE...
"You may m... glories and my ... depose, /But ... my griefs; still ... king of those..."
RICHARD II ...

SAD S...
"For Go... upon the gro... stories of th..."
RIC...

THE COMEDY OF ERRORS

WILD-GOOSE CHASE
"I to the world am like a drop of water / That in the ocean seeks another drop"
ANTIPHOLUS OF SYRACUSE 1.2

STRANGE BEDFELLOWS
"O villain, thou hast stolen both mine office and my name"
DROMIO OF EPHESUS 3.1

DOUBLE, DOUBLE
"I see two husbands, or mine eyes deceive me"
ADRIANA 5.1

ANTIPHOLUS of Syracuse and his servant Dromio arrive in Ephesus. They do not realize their identical twins live in the city as they were separated at birth. After much confusion the two sets of twins finally meet each other and all ends happily.

STAR-CROSSED lovers Romeo and Juliet wed in secret because their families are caught up in a feud. Romeo kills Juliet's cousin and is then banished from Verona. Romeo believes Juliet has died so drinks a deadly poison. When Juliet wakes to find Romeo dead she stabs herself in despair.

WHAT'S IN A NAME?
"My only love sprung from my only hate!"
JULIET 1.5

ROM...

WRETCHED REIGN
"For yet may England curse my wretched reign"
HENRY VI 4.9

LOVE'S LABOUR'S LOST

PROMISE-BREAKER
"O, these are barren tasks, too hard to keep, / Not to see ladies, study, fast, not sleep!"
BIRON 1.1

MOCKING WENCHES
"A lover's eyes will gaze an eagle blind"
BIRON 4.3

THE King of Navarre and his friends vow to avoid the company of women so they can study for three years. Once they meet the Princess of France and her friends they break their oath and the women agree to marry the men, as long as they wait a year and a day for them.

LOGGER-HEADED
"Ill met by moonlight, proud Titania"
OBERON 2.1

MIDSUM...

DEAD AS A DOORNAIL
"I'll make my heaven to dream upon the crown"
RICHARD OF GLOUCESTER 3.2

ONE FELL SWOOP
"At the twelvemonth's end / I'll change my black gown for a faithful friend"
MARIA 5.2

KING Henry agrees for York to become king after he dies, but Margaret kills York. Henry is imprisoned by York's son, Edward, and his other son, Richard, kills him in an attempt to steal the crown for himself.

TWO SETS of human lovers flee to the forest where the King and Queen of the Fairies are fighting. King of the Fairies, Oberon, plays a trick on Titania, the Queen, making her fall in love with a human who has been magically transformed into a donkey. All ends happily with three weddings.

Shakespeare publishes his epic poem *Venus and Adonis* based on Ovid's *Metamorphoses*, Book 10.

1593
London's public playhouses are closed for more than a year due to plague.

1594
Shakespeare jointly founds an acting company called the Lord Chamberlain's Men.

Walter Raleigh sets off on his expedition to South America in a bid to find the "City of Gold", later known as the legendary city of El Dorado.

1595

RICHARD II

SORROW STRUCK
"My soul is full of woe / That blood should sprinkle me to make me grow"
HENRY IV 5.6

...ORIES
...'s sake, let us sit ...und / And tell sad ...e death of kings"
...HARD II 3.2

KING JOHN

BLOODY-MINDED
"He shall not live"
HUBERT 3.1

FOUL PLAY
"Must you with hot irons burn out both mine eyes?"
ARTHUR 4.1

UNHAPPY citizens believe King John's nephew, Arthur, should be king. John orders Hubert to kill Arthur but Hubert allows Arthur to flee. Unluckily, Arthur falls from a high wall during his escape and dies. One of John's enemies poisons him and he dies a horrible death.

PIGEON-LIVERED
"All my bowels crumble up to dust"
JOHN 5.7

EO AND JULIET

STAR-CROSSED LOVERS
"O Romeo, Romeo, wherefore art thou Romeo?"
JULIET 2.2

TALE OF SUCH WOE
"O true apothecary! / Thy drugs are quick. Thus with a kiss I die"
ROMEO 5.1

THE MERCHANT OF VENICE

COLD COMFORT
"I'll have my bond"
SHYLOCK 3.3

THE GAME IS UP
"All that glisters is not gold"
THE PRINCE OF MOROCCO 2.7

FROSTY-SPIRITED
"Shed thou no blood"
PORTIA 4.1

FALSE FACE
"Socks, foul stocking greasy napkins"
FALSTAFF 3.3

BASSANIO wishes to marry Portia but needs to borrow money. His friend Antonio borrows the money from Shylock in exchange for a pound of flesh if he cannot repay him. Antonio cannot pay Shylock back but as the contract does not allow for any blood to be shed he is saved.

...ER NIGHT'S DREAM

HARE-BRAINED
"What angel wakes me from my flowery bed?"
TITANIA 3.1

RARE VISION
"I have had a most rare vision"
BOTTOM 4.1

HENRY IV (PART 1)

TOO MUCH OF A GOOD THING
"You starveling, you elf-skin, you dried neat's tongue, you bull's pizzle, you stock-fish!"
FALSTAFF 2.5

TONGUE-TIED
"For thou hast lost thy princely privilege / With vile participation"
HENRY IV 3.2

SHOOTING STAR
"Thou hast redeemed thy lost opinion"
HENRY IV 5.4

CLAUDIO and... rebellious D... thinking Her... discarded Hero, Cla... Hero's father says h... marries a woman o... revealed to be alive...

KING Henry worries that his wayward son, Hal, won't be a worthy king. Henry faces a rebellion from his people and orders Hal to help him in battle. Hal proves to be a brave soldier, crushing the revolt.

Dutch explorers begin the colonization of the East Indies, leading to the spread of European influence through the Eastern hemisphere.

1596

Shakespeare's father John is granted his own coat of arms, giving him and his son the status of "gentlemen."

Shakespeare's son Hamnet dies aged 11.

1597

Anglo-Dutch forces capture the Spanish city of Cádiz, leading to Spain declaring bankruptcy the following year.

Shakespeare buys New Place, the second largest property in Stratford.

HENRY IV (PART 2)

FAST AND LOOSE

"He hath eaten [m]e out of house and home"
MISTRESS QUICKLY 2.1

BUZZ BUZZ

"Uneasy lies the head that wears a crown"
HENRY IV 3.1

BEFORE WE PROCEED

"I know thee not, old man"
HENRY V 5.5

KING Henry and his son, Hal, are not seeing eye to eye once more. The king grows weak with illness and rebellion spreads. Hal realizes the responsibility of being king and reconciles with Henry. Henry dies and Hal is crowned Henry V.

THE MERRY WIVES OF WINDSOR

ALAS, I AM A WOMAN

"There is no woman's gown big enough for him"
MISTRESS PAGE 4.2

OLD CUCKOLD

"I am made an ass"
FALSTAFF 5.5

SIR JOHN Falstaff attempts to woo two wealthy married women. Mistress Page and Frank Ford plan a series of tricks to humiliate him. After throwing Falstaff in the Thames, dressing him as a woman, and frightening him with friends dressed as fairies, they eventually reconcile and dine together as friends.

MUCH ADO ABOUT NOTHING

Hero are to be married but [Do]n John tricks Claudio into [believing she] has betrayed him. Having [been shamed, Clau]dio believes her to have died. [Hero's father] will forgive Claudio if he [marries a bride of] his choosing. Hero is then [alive and we]ll and they marry after all.

SIGH NO MORE

"Another Hero!"
CLAUDIO 5.4

TRUTH WILL OUT

"Men were deceivers ever"
BALTHASAR 2.3

SOMETHING IS ROTTEN

"Give not this rotten orange to your friend"
CLAUDIO 4.1

AS YOU LIKE IT

NIMBLE-FOOTED

"What think you of falling in love?"
ROSALIND 1.2

WORDS, WORDS, WORDS

"Men have died from time to time, and worms have eaten them, but not for love"
ROSALIND 4.1

FOREVER AND A DAY

"All the world's a stage, And all the men and women merely players"
JAQUES 2.7

ROSALIND falls in love with Orlando. Her wicked uncle banishes her and threatens Orlando's life. Rosalind flees for safety and disguises herself as a boy. Eventually, she reveals her true self to Orlando and they get married in the forest.

JULIUS CAESAR

FOREGONE CONCLUSION

"Beware the ides of March"
SOOTHSAYER 1.2

DASH TO PIECES

"Et tu, Brute?"
CAESAR 3.1

DOGS OF WAR

"Friends, Romans, countrymen, lend me your ears"
MARK ANTONY 3.2

JULIUS CAESAR is more popular than ever with the Roman citizens. His friends, Brutus and Cassius, fearful of his power, plot against him and assassinate him. Another politician, Mark Antony, turns the people against Brutus and a war begins. Brutus is defeated and takes his own life.

SHAKESPEARE TIME

Shakespeare is listed as principal "comedian" in Ben Jonson's play *Every Man in His Humour*, showing that he was a working actor as well as a playwright.

1598

King Henry IV of France issues the Edict of Nantes, granting religious toleration to Protestant reformers and marking the end of the French Wars of Religion.

1599

The Globe Theatre opens on the south bank of the River Thames in London. It is constructed using timber from a previous theater in Shoreditch. Shakespeare becomes a shareholder.

Julius Caesar is one of the first Shakespeare plays to be performed at the Globe Theatre.

HAMLET

A SORRY SIGHT

"Revenge his foul and most unnatural murder"
GHOST 1.5

SNAIL-PACED

"To be, or not to be, that is the question"
HAMLET 3.1

TROILUS AND CRESSIDA

HENRY V

HIGH TIME

"Tennis balls, my liege"
EXETER 1.2

BAND OF BROTHERS

TRIPPINGLY ON THE TONGUE

"Once more unto the breach, dear friends, once more"
HENRY V 3.1

"Is it possible dat I sould love de ennemie of France?"
KATHERINE 5.2

HAND IN HAND

" I tell thee, I am mad / In Cressid's love"
TROILUS 1.1

GREEK TO ME

"Ah, poor our sex! this fault in us I find, / The error of our eye directs our mind"
CRESSIDA 5.2

N EWLY crowned Henry V claims an ancient right to the French throne to exert his power. France and England go to war and Henry leads his troops to a decisive victory at Agincourt. Henry marries the French Princess Katherine to secure peace.

T ROILUS, a Trojan prince, falls in love with Cressida but she is sent to live with the Greeks as part of a hostage exchange. Greek soldier Diomedes woos Cressida, breaking Troilus's heart. In the end, Hector, Troilus's brother, is killed by the Greeks.

TWELFTH NIGHT

OTHELLO

O SPIRIT OF LOVE

"If music be the food of love, play on"
ORSINO 1.1

LAUGHING STOCK

"Some are born great, some achieve greatness, and some have greatness thrust upon 'em" MALVOLIO 2.5

CONSANGUINEOUS

"How have you made division of yourself?"
ANTONIO 5.1

DEVIL INCARNATE

"The Moor already changes with my poison"
IAGO 3.3

GREEN-EYED JEALOUSY

"Do it not with poison, strangle her in her bed"
IAGO 4.1

S HIPWRECKED Viola disguises herself as a boy called Cesario. Olivia, thinking Viola is a man, falls in love with her but Viola is in love with Orsino. Malvolio also loves Olivia and is tricked into wearing yellow stockings to try and woo her. Viola's twin brother appears and, thinking he is Viola, Olivia marries him. Viola reveals she is a girl and marries Orsino, ending the confusion.

LINE STICKERBOOK

1600

E I Co

The East India Company is founded by Elizabeth I. It eventually rules large areas of India with its own private armies.

1601

The Earl of Essex is executed in the Tower of London after plotting against the Queen.

1602

Glovemaker John Shakespeare, William's father, dies.

THE GHOST of Hamlet's father says he was murdered by King Claudius. Hamlet is unsure whether to seek revenge. Claudius arranges a duel with Hamlet, poisoning his sword. Hamlet finally kills Claudius but he is also mortally wounded.

GOODNIGHT, SWEET PRINCE
"The rest is silence"
HAMLET 5.2

TIMON OF ATHENS

SHORT SHRIFT
"Senseless of expense"
FLAVIUS 2.2

FALSE FRIENDS
"Uncover, dogs, and lap"
TIMON 3.7

TIMON lavishes money on his friends but when his money is all gone, they desert him. Timon feeds them a meal of stones to punish them. He goes to live in the woods but finds a pile of gold. His friends return and Timon throws rocks at them, disgusted by their greed.

COLD-BLOODED
"I am Misanthropos, and hate mankind"
TIMON 4.3

KING LEAR

GOOD RIDDANCE
"Which of you shall we say doth love us most"
KING LEAR 1.1

KING LEAR banishes his daughter Cordelia and gives his kingdom to his two other daughters. They betray him, driving him mad. Cordelia returns but is captured and hanged. Her sisters both perish and Lear dies of a broken heart.

MEASURE FOR MEASURE

SEND HIM PACKING
"The venom'd vengeance ride upon our swords"
TROILUS 5.1

COLD AS ANY STONE
"Some rise by sin, and some by virtue fall"
ESCALUS 2.1

DEVOID OF PITY
"O it is excellent / To have a giant's strength; but it is tyrannous / To use it like a giant"
ISABELLA 2.2

AS GOOD LUCK WOULD HAVE IT
"What's mine is yours and what is yours is mine"
THE DUKE 5.1

THE DUKE of Vienna hands power to his deputy, Angelo, and spies on him. Isabella asks Angelo to spare her brother's life. He agrees but only if she agrees to love him. The Duke tricks Angelo into sparing Claudio and proposes to Isabella.

ROMAN soldier Antony is in love with Egyptian Queen, Cleopatra. But when Antony is defeated in battle he blames Cleopatra and vows to kill her. Fearing for her life, Cleopatra pretends she is dead. Antony stabs himself in grief, after which Cleopatra kills herself with a poisonous snake.

ANTONY A

LIE LOW
"I am dying, Egypt, dying"
ANTONY 4.15

SALAD DAYS
"If it be love indeed, tell me how much"
CLEOPATRA 1.1

OTHELLO has secretly married Desdemona. Othello's jealous officer Iago tricks him into thinking Desdemona is in love with another man. Driven crazy with jealousy Othello smothers her in their bed and kills himself.

HOT-BLOODED
"One that loved not wisely but too well"
OTHELLO 5.2

ALL'S WELL THAT ENDS WELL

FOOL'S PARADISE
"Our remedies oft in ourselves do lie"
HELENA 1.1

FANCY-FREE
"A young man married is a man that's marr'd"
PAROLES 2.3

COUNT Bertram is made to marry Helena by the King of France. After they are wed, Bertram refuses to love her unless she fulfills impossible tasks, then flees to Italy. Helena cleverly completes the tasks and Bertram has no choice but to be a good husband.

THEREBY HANGS A TALE
"All's well that ends well; still the fine's the crown"
HELENA 4.4

MACBE

LEND ME YOUR EARS
"Fair is foul, and foul is fair"
WITCHES 1.1

NIGHT OWL
"Is this a dagger which I see before m
MACBETH

1603
Queen Elizabeth I dies after reigning

1604
Scottish King James VI accedes to the throne of England and is crowned James I.
Dr. Faustus, a play in which a man sells his soul to the devil, is first published 11 years after the

1605

1606
Guy Fawkes and his co-conspirators hatch a plot to blow up the Houses of Parliament in Westminster.

DEEPER WRINKLES

CRACK OF DOOM

"Why should a dog, a horse, a rat have life, / And thou no breath at all?"
LEAR 5.3

...flies to wanton ...are we to the gods. ...y kill us for their sport"
GLOUCESTER 4.1

...ND CLEOPATRA

PERICLES

PERICLES'S wife, Thaisa, is thought to have died during childbirth at sea so she is thrown overboard. Pericles leaves his daughter, Marina, to be raised by friends. Years later he is told Marina has died, but eventually they are reunited. Finally, Pericles visits a temple and finds the wife he thought he buried at sea.

THAT WAY MADNESS LIES

"One sorrow never comes but brings an heir"
CLEON 1.4

IN THE TWINKLING OF AN EYE

"Did you ever dream of such a thing?"
A GENTLEMAN 4.5

BAG AND BAGGAGE

"If I should tell / My history it would seem like lies"
MARINA 5.1

POSTHUMUS gives Imogen a bracelet before going to Rome. His enemy Iachimo steals the bracelet, making Posthumus believe Imogen has been unfaithful, so he orders her death. Imogen flees but they are reunited when Posthumus learns of Iachimo's deceit.

WOE IS ME

"With thy sharp teeth this knot intrinsicate / Of life at once untie"
CLEOPATRA 5.2

TOWER OF STRENGTH

"Brave death outweighs bad life"
CORIOLANUS 1.6

CORIOLANUS

UP IN ARMS

"There is a world elsewhere"
CORIOLANUS 3.3

WHAT THE DICKENS!

"O mother, mother! / What have you done?"
CORIOLANUS 5.3

PROSPERO conjures a storm which shipwrecks his evil brother. His magical servant Ariel plays tricks on the castaways. Eventually, Prospero reconciles with his brother and they sail home to Italy.

OUTRAGEOUS FORTUNE

"Your tale, sir, would cure deafness"
MIRANDA...

WAR HERO Coriolanus wants to become a politician but Brutus and Sicinius turn the people against him. Coriolanus goes to live with the enemy. His mother begs him to relent and save Rome. He agrees but is eventually killed by Rome's enemies.

THREE WITCHES tell Macbeth that he will be king of Scotland. His wife convinces him to kill King Duncan and be crowned in his place. The dead king's supporters storm the castle camouflaged with trees and kill Macbeth, putting his head on a spike.

LEONTES believes his wife, Hermione, is pregnant by another man. The baby is banished and Leontes is told Hermione died in childbirth. After sixteen years Leontes and his daughter are reunited and a statue of the late Queen Hermione magically comes to life.

THE WINTER'S TALE

DISH FIT FOR THE GODS

"Exit, pursued by a bear"
STAGE DIRECTION 3.3

OUT OF THE JAWS OF DEATH

"'Tis time; descend; be stone no more"
PAULINA 5.3

ARCITE and Palamon f... love with Emilia thro... their prison window. ... is released and Palamon ma... to escape. The men duel to w... Emilia's love. Arcite wins, b... then dies, leaving Palamon t... marry Emilia. With his final... breath, Arcite blesses the un...

MORE FOOL YOU

"Double, double, toil and trouble, / Fire burn, and cauldron bubble"
WITCHES 4.1

GREEN-EYED MONSTER

"Paddling palms and pinching fingers"
LEONTES 1.2

The Union Jack is adopted as the national maritime flag of Great Britain.

1607

Hamlet is performed on board an East India Company ship called the *Red Dragon*, anchored off the coast of West Africa. This is the first performance of a Shakespeare play on the African continent.

1608

Mary Arden, Shakespeare's mother, dies.

1609

Galileo reports his discovery of moons orbiting Jupiter, providing visible proof that the Earth is not at the center of the universe.

CYMBELINE

SUCH SWEET SORROW
"For my sake wear this; / It is a manacle of love"
POSTHUMUS 1.1

MORE HAIR THAN WIT
"Why did you throw your wedded lady from you?"
IMOGEN 5.5

RANCOROUS SPITE
"I thought her / As chaste as unsunned snow"
POSTHUMUS 2.5

THE TEMPEST

CHARMED LIFE
"O brave new world / That hath such people in't"
MIRANDA 5.1

BRAVE NEW WORLD
"Our revels now are ended ... We are such stuff / As dreams are made on"
PROSPERO 4.1

SHAKESPEARE'S THEATRE
~KEY~
C - COMEDY
H - HISTORY
T - TRAGEDY

THE TWO NOBLE KINSMEN

SLINGS AND ARROWS
"I shall live / To knock thy brains out with my shackles"
PALAMON 2.2

HUMAN KINDNESS
"Take Emilia / And with her all the world's joy"
ARCITE 5.6

SINGLE SPIES
"Of all flowers / Methinks a rose is best"
EMILIA 2.2

HENRY VIII wants to divorce his wife, Katherine, and marry Anne Boleyn. He gets his divorce in spite of Cardinal Wolsey's double-dealing. Katherine has visions of angels on her deathbed. Anne gives birth to the future Queen Elizabeth I.

HENRY VIII (ALL IS TRUE)

TETCHY AND WAYWARD
"I would not be a queen / For all the world"
ANNE BOLEYN 2.5

MAD-HEADED
"They promised me eternal happiness, / And brought me garlands"
KATHERINE 4.2

THE QUEEN'S ENGLISH
"She shall be, to the happiness of England, / An aged princess"
CRANMER 5.4

Shakespeare's final solo-authored work *The Tempest* is completed. The play's hero, Prospero, breaks his magic staff saying goodbye to his enchanted power: could this be Shakespeare's farewell to the stage?

Ireland begins to be settled by English and Scottish Protestants.

The Globe goes up in flames after a cannon misfires during a performance of *Henry VIII*, igniting the wooden beams and thatch. No one is hurt – although one man's breeches have to be put out with a bottle of ale. A new Globe Theatre is built the following year.

610   1611   1612   1613

SHAKESPEARE TIMELINE STICKERBOOK

This stickerbook belongs to:

....

....

How to use the Shakespeare Timeline Stickerbook

What on Earth? Stickerbooks tell giant stories using stickers on a timeline.
To make your own Shakespeare stickerbook, unfold the timeline and put
the stickers from the following pages in the correct places.
Once you have finished, carefully tear the timeline along
the perforated edge and stick it up on the wall

You can also color in our William Shakespeare illustration, which you will find
on the other side of this page.

Color in William Shakespeare!

How many characters can you find? Can you guess who they are?

Shakespeare's Histories

RICHARD III

GHOST OF QUEEN ANNE

JOAN OF ARC

RICHARD II

PRINCE HAL

HENRY IV

THE BUTCHER

HENRY V

HENRY VI & MARGARET

HENRY VI

KING JOHN

HUBERT THE EXECUTIONER

DUKE OF YORK

QUEEN MARGARET

HUBERT & ARTHUR

HENRY VIII & ANNE BOLEYN

FALSTAFF

Shakespeare's Tragedies

TIMON

ANTONY

CORIOLANUS

BAT

JULIET ON BALCONY

GHOST OF HAMELT'S FATHER

ROMEO & JULIET

KING LEAR

DIOMEDES & CRESSIDA

OTHELLO

THREE WITCHES

MARK ANTONY

LAVINIA

RAT

BRUTUS

GHOST OF JULIUS CASEAR

TAMORA & TITUS

ANTONY & CLEOPATRA

MACBETH & LADY MACBETH

Shakespeare's Comedies

BERTRAM

CRAB THE DOG

LEONTES

KING OF NAVARRE

CLAUDIO & HERO

BOTTOM

OLIVIA

KING OF NAVARRE

FOREST FAIRY

ORLANDO

ANTIPHOLUS & DROMIO

PUCK

PRINCESS OF FRANCE

FRANK FORD

PETRUCHIO

OBERON

TITANIA

SHYLOCK & ANTONIO

PERICLES, THAISA AND MARINA

IMOGEN

BEAR

HERMIONE

PROSPERO

ARCITE

DUKE OF VIENNA & ISABELLA

TITANIA & INDIAN PRINCE

PROTEUS & JULIA

ANTIPHOLUS, DROMIO & ADRIANA

PROSPERO

PALAMON

POSTHUMUS

MALVOLIO

FALSTAFF

Shakespeare's Props

WOLF

JOAN OF ARC'S FLAG

TIMON'S TREASURE

RICHARD III'S TENT

FLAG OF WARWICKSHIRE

BOAR'S HEAD INN

MAN ON FIRE

WILLIAM SHAKESPEARE

CLEOPATRA'S MONUMENT

SHORN SHEEP

SEVERED HAND

EYEBALL JAR

ROCK

PROPS DEPT. SIGN

PROPS DEPT.

MUSIC & SOUND

MUSIC & SOUND

GRAVESTONE

IN MEMORY OF
HERO
WHO DIED ON THE
15TH DAY
OF MAY 1598
AGED 15 YEARS

DOG ON WHEELS

HOUSE MUSICIANS

DRESS

CASTLE TURRET

SUITCASE

CANNON

VULTURE

SCENERY PAINTING

LAUNDRY BASKET

BEAR RUG

WITCHES' CAULDRON

SHAKESPEARE'S
the Bards
HOUSE BAND

BASS DRUM

Shakespeare's Life & Times

LORD CHAMBERLAIN'S MEN

VENUS AND ADONIS

WALTER RALEIGH

SHAKESPEARE'S POEM

CHRISTOPHER MARLOWE

THE GLOBE

PRINCIPAL 'COMEDIAN'

PLAGUE DOCTOR

YOUNG SHAKESPEARE

EDICT OF NANTES

RIALTO BRIDGE

QUEEN ELIZABETH

KING JAMES

COAT OF ARMS

EXECUTION OF ESSEX

GALILEO

GLOVEMAKER

ANGLO-DUTCH FORCES CAPTURE CADIZ

MARY ARDEN

JULIUS CAESAR

EAST INDIA COMPANY

GUY FAWKES

THE TEMPEST

UNION JACK

EAST INDI

IRELAND'S FIRST SETTLERS

FIRE

NEDERLANDSCH OOST INDIE

THE STICKERBOOK TIMELINE COLLECTION

OUR TIMELINES COME IN THREE FABULOUS FORMATS:

WALLBOOKS feature a six-foot timeline, plus a newspaper packed with stories, pictures, letters and a quiz. Perfect for everyone aged 6–106.

STICKERBOOKS each have around a hundred stickers and a five-foot simplified version of the timeline to stick them on to. Perfect for younger readers.

POSTERBOOKS are gigantic ten-foot versions of the timeline, printed on heavy paper and laminated for extra durability. Perfect for schools.

1. Nature **2.** Science **3.** Big History **4.** Shakespeare

Published by What on Earth Publishing Ltd in association with the Shakespeare Birthpace Trust.
© 2017 All rights reserved. ISBN: 978-0-9955766-8-1

Contact us at info@whatonearthbooks.com or visit whatonearthbooks.com